Unleash Your Creativity with Painting and Drawing

Techniques for All

Table of Contents

Chapter 1. Introduction

Unleash the riot of colors, patterns, and ideas hidden within you with our Special Report: "Unleash Your Creativity with Painting and Drawing: Techniques for All." Offering an exhilarating journey into the world of creativity, this report is brimming with tips, tricks, and techniques that empower anyone—be they novices or seasoned artists—to tap into their artistic potential. Packed with step-by-step guides, expert opinions, and the secrets behind famous art masterpieces, it promises to awaken your creative genius, unlock your imagination, and set it loose onto the canvas of your dreams. Our Special Report is not just an artistic guide—it's your ticket to embark on a transformative, joyful journey that molds the profusion of your thoughts into compelling portraits, landscapes, and abstracts. Let's get those brushes moving, shall we?

Chapter 2. The Artistic Mind: Harnessing Your Inner Creativity

Boldly stepping into the world of artistry begins with an intimate exploration of the self. Utilizing the phenomenal capacity of our brains is key in unlocking the treasure trove of creative potential hidden within us. To begin this journey, it's essential to first understand what creativity is all about—the open dialogue between imagination and reality, a remarkable feat that the human mind is capable of achieving.

Creativity is an invaluable force that enables us to view the world from myriad perspectives, bestowing upon us a spectrum of visual comprehensions that transcend the mundane and ordinary. Using distinctive language, unique pairings, unorthodox patterns, and an unusual amalgamation of forms and shades, creativity helps us communicate our unique visions to the world.

2.1. Understanding the Artistic Mind

Artistic minds are often characterized by a heightened ability to perceive the minutiae of elements that interact to form our world. Far from being a passive observer, an artist's mind ceaselessly seeks connections, patterns, and forms within the chaos of the cosmos, bestowing aesthetic dimensions onto ordinary sights. The famous artist Pablo Picasso once said, "Every child is an artist. The problem is how to remain an artist once he grows up." Picasso's statement throws light on the cultural constructs that often throttle our innate creativity as we grow up.

Your creative self is not something that can be switched on when you wish to draw or paint—it must be a part of your everyday life. Begin by welcoming a non-linear, non-conventional approach to problems, situations, and perspectives. Creative thinking liberates us from the shackles of established norms and encourages us to explore the unfamiliar, thereby igniting our artistic minds.

2.2. Embracing the Chaos

Chaos is an integral part of the path to creativity. Embracing the chaos around and within us paves the way to extraordinary artistic creations. Artists throughout history have turned the tumult of their emotions, thoughts, and experiences into masterpieces that continue to speak to our souls. Gain inspiration from the unpredictable dance of autumn leaves, the mesmerizing patterns in the chaos of a bustling city, even in the disarray of your ideas, and there you'll find a unique piece of art waiting to be born.

2.3. The Creative Process

The creative process is constantly ongoing, even when you aren't holding a paintbrush or sketching pencil. Everything that you observe, learn, experience, and feel contributes to your artistic journey. Many times, it's a meandering path rather than a direct one.

1. Preparation: This is the stage where you gather your material—both physical, like paint or pencils, and mental, in the form of ideas and inspirations. Take notes, sketch quick drafts, collect inspiring images, and immerse yourself in your subject.

2. Incubation: Here, you let your ideas "stew." Think about them, but allow them to evolve and grow in your subconscious.

3. Illumination: It's the "aha!" moment when everything clicks together, and you see a clear path forward for your piece of art.

4. Verification: This is where you experiment with your idea, refining and adjusting it to create the final product.

Respecting each stage of the creative process and giving it its due time is crucial to nurturing your creativity. It's in this process of trial and error, problem-solving and overcoming obstacles, that you'll discover your unique artistic voice.

2.4. Overcoming Creative Blocks

Creative blocks can be frustrating. Remember, everyone faces them somewhere on their creative journey. See them as hurdles you must leap across, not walls that halt your progress. Use exercises such as free writing, creative prompts, and mind maps to stimulate your imagination. Embrace new experiences, and take advantage of the healing power of nature. Practice mindfulness and stay physically active, as they're known to foster creativity.

2.5. Enriching Your Artistic Toolbox

Drawing and painting are talents that require regular practice, dedication, and an ever-expanding toolbox of knowledge and techniques. Experiment with different types of art—abstract, minimalism, realism, surrealism—and with different media like oil paints, watercolors, acrylics, pastels, or pencils, and find what resonates with you.

Each form and medium will bring a different flavor to your creative process and will help you express your unique observations and experiences, thereby allowing you to unlock newer realms of creativity.

2.6. Final Thoughts: Keeping the Creative Spark Alive

Creativity is not a one-time event—it's a lifelong journey. It requires time, practice, and the courage to make mistakes and learn from them. Surround yourself with people who inspire you and evoke positive emotions. Art thrives where there's positive energy, open-mindedness, and awe-inspiring stimuli.

So, journey on. Keep experimenting, keep exploring, and most importantly, keep expressing. Your mind, richly endowed with creativity, holds countless universes waiting to be interpreted and conveyed onto the canvas. Over time, your creativity will become an organic expression of your consciousness, and you will realize that art and life are not separate; they are entwined, forming a beautifully complex tapestry that reflects our human experience.

Chapter 3. Wielding the Tools: A Guide to Art Materials

Painting and drawing, two of the most rudimentary art forms, rely to a large extent on the artist's relationship, understanding, and dexterity with their tools. Primarily, these tools comprise various forms of brushes, paints, canvas, and drawing materials. Having a thorough knowledge of these materials can greatly improve the execution of your artistic ideas. This guide aims to provide meticulous insights into these tools, their usage, and the nuances of choosing them wisely.

3.1. Understanding Brushes

Brushes are quintessential for both painting and drawing. They come in various shapes, sizes, and segments. Brushes are generally classified based on three aspects - shape, size, and the kind of fibers used.

1. **Shape:** There are a variety of brush shapes including round, flat, bright, filbert, fan, and more. Each shape allows for distinctive stroke styles. For instance, Filbert brushes are ideal for blending and creating soft, round edges, while Round brushes provide precision and detail.

2. **Size:** The size of a brush significantly impacts the thickness of the strokes. It's essential to select the brush size that suits the requirement of your sketch or painting. Brushes usually come in sizes ranging from 000, being the smallest, to 20 or over, the largest.

3. **Fiber:** Brushes can be made from natural animal hair or synthetic fibers. Natural brushes are expensive but offer a

smooth application of paint, typically oil or watercolor. Synthetic brushes, whilst cheaper, are more durable and versatile. They work quite well with acrylic paint due to their stiffness and durability.

3.2. Choosing Your Paint

Paint is the element that brings life to your creation. There are numerous types of paints, with each providing a unique finish and texture. Let's dive into some of the most commonly used ones.

1. **Oil Paint:** Known for their vibrant color and slow drying time, oil paints are a beloved medium among artists. This slow drying feature allows artists to tweak their art over time and achieve smooth transitions between colors.

2. **Acrylic Paint:** Acrylic paints are known for their swift drying quality and versatility. They can mimic both oil and watercolor paints and can adhere to a variety of surfaces ranging from canvas to wood and even fabric.

3. **Watercolor:** Watercolor paints provide a translucent, flowing finish. They are ideal for capturing light and creating a sense of movement.

3.3. Canvas Selection

The canvas is to an artist what the stage is to a dancer. It is a silent yet salient participant in your creative journey. Its texture and priming determine how paint behaves.

1. **Canvas Texture:** from coarse to smooth, canvas texture changes the perception of your artwork. Coarse textures are great for visible, bold brush strokes, while smooth surfaces are ideal for detailed work.

2. **Priming:** A canvas usually comes either primed or unprimed.

Priming creates a smooth, ready-to-use surface, and protects the canvas from the acidic nature of paint. Oil painting requires a primed canvas, whilst for acrylics it's optional.

3.4. Pens and Pencils

For the delineation of fine details, or for creating standalone pieces, pens, pencils, and other drawing tools are indispensable. Here's a lowdown on these essential tools.

1. **Pencils:** Their hardness rating affects the darkness of lines. A 'B' rating represents 'soft' or 'black', and an 'H' represents 'hard'. The scale runs from 9H (lightest) to 9B (darkest). Take your pick depending on the desired effect.

2. **Pens:** While pens may seem straightforward, there are varieties from which to choose. From fountain pens that offer a unique flow of ink, to ballpoint pens that may be easier to maneuver, every artist has their favorite. Experiment with several types until you find your preferred writing instrument.

3. **Charcoal:** Charcoal is used for its deep, black lines and ease with shading and creating texture. It comes in a variety of forms ranging from pencils, sticks to compressed blocks.

3.5. Paper and Its Role

While canvas often takes precedence, paper also contributes considerably to the outcome of a painting or drawing. Paper quality, texture, and weight all play roles in how the final artwork appears.

1. **Quality:** Acid-free paper is advisable for long-lasting works as it doesn't yellow with time. For watercolors, paper should have a high cotton content to facilitate water absorption.

2. **Texture:** Texture influences how mediums react to the paper. Rough textures can create interesting effects with drawing tools

whilst smooth paper is preferred for detailed works.

3. **Weight:** Heavier weight paper prevents the paper from warping when wet mediums like watercolor or acrylics are used. It's measured in GSM (grams per square meter)—the higher the GSM, the heavier the paper.

To conclude, understanding the tools at your disposal is half the battle in the creation of art. Experimentation is key, and this guide serves as a first step in identifying the materials you require. The rest, as always, depends on the vast expanse of your imagination.

Chapter 4. The Language of Lines: Mastering Drawings

Lines are the very essence of drawings. They are the fundamental building blocks, the atoms, if you will, of an artist's work. They with their simple essence can represent complex forms, create depth, give a sense of movement or emotion, and dictate the viewer's gaze.

4.1. Understanding the Role of Lines in Drawing

Before one takes to mastering control over lines, it is crucial to understand their role in an artwork. Lines perform a multitude of functions. They could be the contour that defines the silhouette of a subject or the hatching that infuses it with a sense of light and shadow.

Imagine a still life composition in front of you—a bowl of fruits on a table. If you were to draw it, the boundary of each fruit, the tabletop, the edges of the bowl; each of these contours would be defined by a line. These are the very bones of your drawing.

But lines do not stop there. Notice the orange basking in the warm light? The side away from the light source is crinkled into shadows while the nearer side is illuminated. How would you represent this play of light? That's where hatching and cross-hatching with lines come into play.

4.2. Tips and Techniques: Controlling Your Line

Mastering the art of drawing begins with controlling your line. The pressure of your pencil against the sketch pad, the speed of your stroke, the symmetry of your curves; every minute factor contributes to the final locus of your line.

1. Warm-up with Loose Lines: Begin your drawing session with some loose lines, swirls, and scribbles to warm up your hand. Do fast loops, slow, sweeping lines, angular patterns, or just freeform squiggles. This exercise frees up your muscles and helps ease any tension or stiffness.

2. Variable Line Weight: To add interest and depth to your drawing, use variable line weight. This implies altering the heaviness and thinness of your lines within a single drawing. Typically, heavier lines are used to indicate shadow, bring specific elements to the forefront, create an illusion of depth, or imply a change in plane. Lighter lines are often used for highlights or to create a sense of distance.

3. Utilizing the Pencil: Stay aware of your pencil and its angle. When held at a sharp angle, the pencil lends itself to precise, thin lines which are perfect for detailed work. In contrast, when held at a low angle, it gives broader strokes, perfect for shading and creating texture.

4.3. Learning Techniques: Hatching and Cross Hatching

One of the most intriguing aspects of drawing with lines is the creation of tone and texture through hatching and cross-hatching. In essence, these are simple techniques wherein lines are drawn close together to build up regions of light and dark.

1. Hatching: Hatching involves drawing parallel lines close together. The closer the lines, the darker the area appears. The exact nature of hatching can vary with the change in direction, length, closeness, and curvature of lines.

2. Cross Hatching: This is similar to hatching, but involves drawing another set of lines over the first, intersecting them at an angle. This forms a dense network of lines and creates deeper tones.

In both these techniques, understanding the direction of lines is crucial. The lines should follow the form of the object. The more effectively you do this, the more three-dimensional your drawing becomes.

4.4. Decoding the Type of Lines

It's not just about control and technique, it's also about understanding the different types of lines and what they can represent or convey.

1. Straight Lines: These are the basic constructs, primarily used to define and outline shapes and objects. They form the skeletal structure in most sketches.

2. Curved Lines: These aid in depicting organic and natural forms. They also help in expressiveness, detailing, and softening the overall effect.

3. Zigzag Lines: These are primarily used to denote a change or interruption, often used symbolically or to represent specific textures, such as fabric or fur.

4. Dotted or Dashed Lines: They typically represent interim, non-solid, or unseen lines.

Understanding the language of lines is a constant journey of exploration and practice. The wealth of what can be achieved with simple lines is astounding. From invoking emotions to creating illusions, this basic art element holds unlimited potential. So, as you pick up your pencil today and let it glide across the paper, remember, you're doing more than drawing - you're speaking in the silent but powerful language of lines.

Chapter 5. Poetry of Colors: Understanding Color Theory

Colors are the syntax of the visible world, an alphabet that each of us has learned to read from our earliest age. It is a language that is both universal and profoundly personal—an emotional vocabulary that we use to express our identities, to articulate our desires and fears, to embellish our memories, and to shape our hopes. When you pick up a palette, you are not just choosing between different hues but between the multifarious voices and visions of color.

5.1. The Science of Color

We perceive colors as the result of light interacting with our eyes. Light from a source (like the sun, a lightbulb, or an LED screen) is either transmitted directly to our eyes, or it bounces off an object and then enters our eyes. The 'color' of an object that we perceive is merely the wavelength of light that is reflected by it and not absorbed.

The color spectrum that human beings can see ranges from red, with the longest wavelength, to violet, with the shortest. When all colors come together, we see white light. And, interestingly, when no light is perceived, we see black.

5.2. Primary, Secondary, and Tertiary Colors

In color theory, we talk about primary, secondary, and tertiary colors. These terms describe relational characteristics of colors.

- Primary colors: In traditional color theory, primary colors are the foundational colors that cannot be created by mixing other colors. The primary colors are red, blue, and yellow. These colors can be combined to create all other colors.

- Secondary colors: These are the colors obtained by mixing equal amounts of primary colors. The secondary colors are green (a mix of blue and yellow), orange (a mix of yellow and red), and purple (a mix of red and blue).

- Tertiary colors: These are created by combining a primary color with an adjacent secondary color. Examples include red-orange (red + orange), yellow-green (yellow + green), and blue-purple (blue + purple).

5.3. The Color Wheel

The color wheel is an invaluable tool for understanding and visualizing how different colors relate to each other. It gives us a framework to understand the relationships between primary, secondary, and tertiary colors. The standard color wheel has 12 segments: three primary colors, three secondary, and six tertiary colors.

The color wheel also helps us understand complementary colors. These are colors that are opposite each other on the color wheel. When used together, complementary colors create dynamic and high contrast color schemes. Examples include red and green, blue and orange, or yellow and purple.

5.4. Warm Colors and Cool Colors

Colors can also be classified as either warm or cool. This distinction is less concrete and more subjective, with certain cultures or times assigning different temperatures to the same colors.

- Warm colors: Colors like red, orange, and yellow are typically associated with warmth and are therefore classified as 'warm colors'. They can evoke feelings of warmth, comfort, passion, or even aggression.

- Cool colors: Colors like blue, green, and violet are classified as 'cool colors'. These colors are often associated with calmness, relaxation, and nature. They can evoke feelings of peace, tranquility, and sometimes sadness.

5.5. Color Schemes and Harmony

Harmony is the pleasing arrangement of parts. In color theory, we refer to harmonious color combinations as color schemes. Here are a few commonly used color schemes:

- Monochromatic: Monochromatic color schemes use different tints, shades, and tones within a particular hue. This creates a cohesive and elegant palette, but can feel monotonous if not used properly.

- Analogous: Analogous color schemes are created by picking colors that are next to each other on the color wheel. This creates a serene and comforting scheme, but with more variety than a monochromatic scheme.

- Complementary: Complementary color schemes are created by pairing colors opposite each other on the color wheel. This creates high contrast and a vibrant look.

- Triadic: Triadic color schemes use three colors equally spaced around the color wheel. This creates a balanced and harmonious look.

It's important to note that no single color scheme is inherently superior to others. It's the artist's understanding of the relationships, harmony, and the emotions that colors can evoke, that brings life to their work. Through a combination of craft and intuition, color becomes a crucial tool for the artist to render their vision on to canvas.

In our forthcoming sections, we will delve deeper into the practical applications of color theory in painting and drawing, and how you can harness this potent syntax to unleash your creativity.

Remember, the pursuit of mastery in color theory, like any artistic endeavor, will be fraught with moments of uncertainty and frustration. But it is these very challenges that will catalyze your growth as an artist. So, be patient with yourself, stay curious, and above all, enjoy the journey as you explore the poetry of colors!

Chapter 6. Step into the Light: Playing with Lighting and Shadows

In the realm of art, light and shadow aren't just added for dramatic effect. They serve as the bedrock of realism and play a pivotal role in conjuring mood, depth, and atmosphere in a piece. Harnessing the profound interplay of these elements can turn a simple sketch into a stunning work of art.

Understanding Light

In order to truly grasp the intricacies of light and shadow, we must first appraise the source of light, its intensity, color, direction, and the manner in which it reflects off of objects.

Light Source: There are two kinds of light sources: direct, like the sun or a lamp, and indirect, such as reflected light bouncing from a wall or floor. A direct light source often creates hard, clear shadows, while an indirect source, due to its diffuse nature, is softer and results in muted, blurred shadows.

Intensity and Color: The intensity and temperature (color) of light impact the painting significantly. High-intensity, cool-toned light tends to produce sharp, cool shadows with warm, bright highlights. Meanwhile, lower intensity, warm light results in softer shadows and less contrast between light and shadow.

Direction: The direction from which light falls on your subject dictates the shape and depth of shadows. Light from different directions gives different effects. Side lighting emphasizes texture, backlights create silhouettes, while top lighting can give a three-dimensional feel.

Reflections: Understanding reflected light and how it influences the color and tone of shadows is key in depicting how objects interact with their surroundings in a realistic painting.

6.1. Learn to See the Light

When studying the play of light and shadow, squint your eyes at the scene. By doing so, you will blur the details and can concentrate on the larger areas of light and dark without distraction. You can then convert those into shapes that would be more manageable on canvas.

6.2. Start with Monochrome Studies

Monochrome studies, or value sketches, allow you to play around with light and shadow without the added complexity of color. This technique requires you to observe the light and dark areas in a scene and render them in varying shades of the same color. It can prove invaluable as it teaches how the distribution of lights, mid-tones, and darks create a sense of depth and volume.

6.3. Mastering Shadows

One common mistake artists make is to depict shadows as simple darker forms of the object's color. In reality, shadows are filled with color and varying degrees of light or dark, depending on factors like the angle and quality of your light source.

Chapter 7. Cast Shadows

Cast shadows are shadows that form when light is blocked by an object. They are crisper near the object casting the shadow and become blurry as they move away from it. Observing these shadows closely and practicing their nuances can help you portray depth convincingly. Remember, the color of cast shadows will be affected by reflected light from the surrounding environment.

7.1. Form Shadows

When light falls on an object, the part of the object facing away from the light forms what is known as a form shadow. These shadows are used to render the object's three-dimensional form.

Form shadows transition from the core shadow (the darkest part of the shadow, furthest from the light source) to the reflected light and finally to the lightest part known as the highlight.

Always remember that form shadows should appear softer and lighter compared to cast shadows as they include reflected light within them.

7.2. Playing with Contrast

Contrast is, simply put, the difference between light and dark areas in your composition. Tugging at the contrast can lend drama to a piece and spotlight the focal point of the artwork. A high contrast between shadows and highlights usually leads to a bold, dynamic composition, while low contrast results in a calm, subtle, and dreamy aura.

7.3. Step by Step Guide to a Simple Light and Shadow Study

Now, let's tie it all together with a step-by-step guide to your first light and shadow study.

1. Select an object or setup to study.

2. Set up your lighting in a controlled environment.

3. Start by sketching the object and scene lightly onto your canvas.

4. Squint your eyes and identify the areas of light and dark.

5. Block in the major areas of light and dark with suitable shades.

6. Gradually, start differentiating the mid-tones, reflected light, core of the shadow, and highlights.

7. Observe the transitions between the light and shadow and blend them appropriately.

By the end of this study, you should have a significantly better grasp of the behavior of light and shadow and be ready to explore more complex subjects.

Light and shadow are fascinating and profound concepts in art, capable of bringing your artworks to life. Studies and practice can help you portray them convincingly and use them effectively to evoke emotions and direct the viewer's attention as desired throughout your piece. Take your time, observe the world around you closely, and never stop learning and experimenting.

Chapter 8. Portraying Reality: Techniques in Still Life and Landscape

From the bountiful fruit baskets meticulously depicted by Caravaggio, to the atmospheric countryside landscapes of Constable, we find ourselves consistently enchanted by the artists' abilities to weave reality onto a canvas. But how can we, too, manage this daunting task? This chapter endeavors to help you unlock the mysteries of painting landscapes and still lifes, sketching reality with your brush, and filling your canvas with life.

8.1. Choosing Your Subject

In still life and landscape painting, the key to authenticity is observation. Begin by selecting a subject that is not only feasibly counted among your painting abilities, but also one that holds your interest. Whether it's a vibrant bowl of fruit or an abandoned barn nestled in a field, the authenticity of your piece starts with a genuine interest in your chosen subject.

8.2. Eye of Observation

The first action is to study your subject keenly. Observe the play of light and shadow, the subtle color variations, the textures, and details. Transferring these observations accurately to your canvas is the crux of still life and landscape painting.

8.3. Composing the Picture

Just as the grammatical rules guide a language, the principles of composition guide painting. The rule of thirds, balance, focus, depth, and perspective all bring stability and structure to your piece, making it not just a depiction, but a visually engaging art.

8.4. Mastering Perspective

Perspective is a fundamental aspect of representational art. Start by identifying the horizon line, vanishing points, and orthogonal lines. Use them to orientate objects in your painting to create depth and volume. The theory behind perspective can feel overwhelming, but with practice, you can master its effect.

8.5. The Play of Light and Shadow

Light and shadow define form. Become adept at understanding the direction, quality, and temperature of light. Consider how these elements impact your subject—forming shadows, creating highlights and mid-tones, determining color harmony, and even the mood of the piece.

8.6. Palette: Your Color Symphony

A harmonious color scheme can make or break a painting. Start with the color wheel to understand complementary and analogous color schemes. Remember, less is more. Begin with a restrictive palette and expand as you grow more confident.

8.7. Brushwork Techniques

Explore various brushwork techniques and textures. Different methods like scumbling, glazing, impasto, etc., can bring your painting to life, adding depth and interest.

8.8. Blocking In

Start by blocking in the main shapes and areas of your painting. This acts as a foundation, enabling you to achieve the primary composition and color scheme of the piece.

8.9. Detailed Work

Once the basic forms are established, you can move on to detailed work. Add textures, create depth, play with light and shadow, incorporate nuances of colors, and breathe life into your painting.

8.10. Finishing Touches

The final touch is often the most crucial step in your work, providing the requisite polish. Add the slightest details, necessary highlights, and the final brush strokes to complete your piece.

8.11. Critically Evaluating Your Work

Take time to step back and critically evaluate your work. Look for areas that need improvements, such as color harmony, depth, composition, and perspective. Remember, the first draft is seldom perfect. Reiterative enhancements are part of the process.

Whether you idealize the rustic charm of a landscape or the quaint charm of a still life, painting and drawing offer a comprehensive way to capture the world around you. With a keen eye, practiced techniques, and above all, an open mind, you can bring your unique vision to life on the canvas. Lap up the colors, drink in the light, and let your portrait of reality transform the silent into the eloquent, the static into the dynamic – let it breathe, beam, and bristle with life. Let your canvas speak the language of your perception.

Chapter 9. Capturing the Human Essence: Basics of Portrait Drawing and Painting

From the curve of a cheekbone to the twinkle in an eye, human faces are an enigma waiting to be unraveled by your artistic spirit. Let's dive deep into understanding the basics of portrait drawing and painting, and begin our journey of recognizing and capturing the essence of human expressions.

9.1. Understanding Face Anatomy

Understanding human face anatomy is the cornerstone of portrait art. Familiarize yourself with its structure—skull, facial muscles, skin texture, and the effects of light and shadow.

First, we outline the "oval" based representation of the face. To visualise this, draw an oval slightly tilting to the side.

[sketch oval face] | *sketch_oval_face.jpg*

Figure 1. Anchor your sketch

Develop this initial sketch further by adding two intersecting lines—the vertical line being the symmetry axis of the face, and a horizontal line indicating the position of the eyes. Over time, you'll realize that the eyes are usually positioned halfway between the top of the head and the chin—the horizontal line indicates this position, acting as a reliable guide.

[head outlines] | *head_outlines.jpg*

Figure 2. Complete the head outlines

9.2. "Breaking" the Face—Dividing into Proportions

One of the secrets of drawing a convincing portrait is correctly applying face proportions. Divide the face into thirds: the top section houses the forehead and hairline, the middle holds the eyebrows to the base of the nose, and the last third extends from the base of the nose to the chin.

Once you're comfortable with the general placement and proportions of the features, you can further break the face down and concentrate on each feature in detail.

9.3. Detailed Focus on Facial Features

Eyes

The human eye is not just a mere window to the soul but also an intricate subject to sketch. Start with an almond-shaped outline for the eyes. Inside the outline, draw a circle for the iris and a smaller one for the pupil. Remember, pupils should not touch the top and bottom eyelid—it contributes towards a more realistic look. Do not forget to leave a small white dot for light reflection to give them life.

Eyebrows

The eyebrows sit on the brow bone—which is also marked by the second horizontal line you drew earlier. They typically start directly above the inside corner of your eye and then arch upwards and outwards, following the eye's curvature.

Nose

The nose can be simplified into three basic shapes: the bridge (a narrow rectangle), the tip or ball of the nose (an oval), and the nostrils (two small circles). The sides of the nostrils line up with the tear ducts of the eyes—with this as your reference, position and draw the nose.

Mouth

The mouth can be split into three parts: the opening (or line) of the mouth and the two lips. Use gentle curves to outline these, remembering that the mouth is wider than the nose. An easy reference point is that the corners of the mouth usually align with the center of each eye.

9.4. Skill of Observation

In portrait art, the skill of observation is as critical as the skill of drawing or painting. Observe your subject closely, noticing how various emotions play on their face—joy narrows the eyes slightly, sadness droops the mouth's corners. Notice how light and shadow define their features, how details like freckles, wrinkles, or dimples add character. Transform your observations into lines and strokes—this breathes life into your portrait.

9.5. Light and Shadow—The Drama Creators

Understanding how light and shadow work is key. They carve the face into a three-dimensional form. The face can be divided into planes that are either facing the light or turning away from it. The lighted planes reflect light, while the shadowed ones absorb it. Use this understanding to apply shadows and highlights in your drawing, making it look convincingly real.

9.6. Expression and Emotion

A good portrait is more than just about the right lines and shadows; it's also about capturing the essence of the subject's emotion. What mood does the face portray—joy, sorrow, surprise, or contemplation? Capturing these ephemeral aspects breathes life into your portraits and makes them resonate with viewers.

9.7. Materials and Tools Choices

Your choice of materials can vastly impact the outcome of your portrait. Pencil sketching, charcoal, or pastel for drawing, oil or acrylic for painting—the medium you choose can bring out unique qualities and enhance the visual impact of the face you wish to capture.

In the end, remember that every face is unique; use these principles as a guide, but adapt as necessary for each new subject. Through persistent practice and keen observation, your ability to capture any face's essence in a portrait will surely flourish. Let your passion guide your hand, and make every stroke count.

Chapter 10. Beyond the Obvious: Exploring Abstract Art

Often dismissed as simply splashes of color or odd geometric shapes, abstract art veers away from visual representations of the world and instead uses form, color, and lines to achieve its artistic intent. To truly appreciate and explore abstract art, one must delve deep into its unique characteristics, learn to understand its principles, and master the techniques associated with this challenging yet rewarding genre.

10.1. An Unbound Artistic Expression

Abstract art stands for freedom—that of the artist and also of the viewer to interpret what they see. This genre doesn't strictly adhere to visual reality but is more of an inner reality expressed through the artist's strokes. The interpretation hinges purely on personal responses, giving viewers the liberty to see and decipher as their emotions dictate.

Let's look at cubism, pioneered by Picasso and Braque, which presents multiple facets of an object simultaneously, regardless of physical impossibility. Surrealism too, residing in the realm of dreams and the unconscious, endeavors to surpass ordinary bounds.

Abstract art throws the doors wide open—to interpretation, to experience, to subjectivity—and it is in this vast, uncharted territory that your creative explorations should begin.

10.2. Techniques to Master

Abstract art welcomes a wide range of techniques that allow you to express your thoughts and emotions freely on the canvas.

1. Experiment with Colors: Abstract art does not demand conformity to natural colors. Feel free to use bold, vibrant colors or settle on more subdued hues, based on the mood or message you wish to convey.

2. Utilize Texture: Create multi-dimensional works by adding materials such as sand, paper, or fabric to your canvas. This not only provides depth but also adds a tactile element to your pieces.

3. Experiment with Scale: Abstract art isn't confined to trivial or life-sized representations. Playing with scale can yield compelling results.

4. Non-Traditional Tools: Think beyond brushes. Use palette knives, sponges, or even your fingers to create unusual effects.

Remember, the key to mastering abstract art is to let go of any preconceived notions and embrace the uncensored outpouring of your creativity.

10.3. Deciphering the Abstract Language

Understanding the language of abstract art is as important as mastering its techniques.

Elements of Art: Familiarize yourself with the basic elements of art, including line, shape, form, color, and texture. These elements can communicate your thoughts, emotions, or concepts in your abstract art.

Principles of Design: Balance, contrast, emphasis, movement, pattern, rhythm, unity—these design principles provide structure for your abstract paintings and help convey your artistic intent.

10.4. Learn from the Masters

Studying the work of abstract masters can provide valuable insights. Kandinsky, Pollock, Mondrian—each has their unique style, spreading across different movements within abstract art. Their works are perfect examples of the principles and techniques we've discussed so far.

10.5. Unleashing Your Creativity

The final and most vital step—getting started.

1. Choose your Medium: Experiment with various mediums like acrylics, oil paints, or watercolors. Each has its distinct properties and can yield different effects.

2. Set your Mood: Abstract art is a reflection of your emotion, thoughts, or concepts. Determining the message or mood you wish to convey can guide your choice of colors, lines, and textures.

3. Get Inspired: Draw inspiration from the world around you, from your thoughts, dreams, or emotions.

4. Experiment, Experiment!: Don't be afraid to make mistakes. Experiment with techniques, colors, shapes, and everything else. Abstract art is all about freedom.

In abstract art, there are no rules except the ones you set for yourself. Each stroke is a footprint of your personal journey, each color a fragment of your emotion, each form a nugget of your thought. You are only limited by your imagination. So, pick up your brush, or fingers, or sponge, and begin your journey into the uncharted territories of your own creativity. After all, the world is but a canvas to our imagination.

Chapter 11. Deciphering Masterpieces: Lessons from Art History

Art masterpieces are treasuries of valuable lessons and insights, offering an unparalleled opportunity for aspiring artists to learn and grow. An in-depth understanding of these stellar creations allows us to unearth the depth of thought, attention to detail, and creative prowess the artists imbued in their work.

11.1. Insights from the Renaissance

The Renaissance period witnessed a radical transformation in art, with the emergence of innovative techniques that lent depth and realism to artistic creations. This period birthed several masterpieces, one of the most iconic pieces being Leonardo da Vinci's 'Mona Lisa.'

'Mona Lisa's enchanting beauty and enigmatic expression are captivating, but what's more interesting is da Vinci's unique technique—sfumato. This method involves delicate blending of colors, creating soft outlines that have an almost 'smoky' appearance. The technique created a sense of depth in the portraits, a feature that made da Vinci's work stand out.

Lessons:

- Patience and precision: Da Vinci's technique was a painstaking process that required meticulous attention to detail and inexhaustible patience.

- Experimentation: The 'sfumato' was a novel technique in that era, and its success lay in da Vinci's fearlessness in experimenting with new methods of expression.

11.2. Influence of Post-Impressionism

Post-impressionists, like Vincent van Gogh, broke off from the realism of Impressionism and introduced more emotional and symbolic representation in their work. His 'Starry Night' with its vibrant, swirling colors and dramatic brush strokes evokes emotion and invites interpretation.

Lessons:

- Expressivity: Van Gogh's work teaches us the importance of expressing our emotions through art. His bold use of color and distinctive brushwork reflect his emotions, making his work resounding and relatable.

11.3. Modern Art and its Abstract Connotations

Modern Art swept across the 19th and 20th centuries, redefining traditional artistic conventions. Picasso's 'Guernica,' a hallmark of symbolism and abstraction, is a riotous evocation of the horrors of war.

Lessons:

- Symbolism: 'Guernica' uses disjointed, deformed figures that symbolize chaos and suffering, showing how symbols can carry strong meanings in a painting.

11.4. The Minimalist Movement

The Minimalist Movement, with artists like Agnes Martin, made simple geometrical patterns and monochrome panels profound modes of expression.

Lessons:

- Simplicity: The minimalist art teaches us that complexity or detailed work is not always necessary to deliver a powerful message. Sometimes, less is indeed more.

Masterpieces offer a treasure trove of techniques, themes, and ideas. They are not just objects of awe and inspiration but can also serve as path-bearers to our artistic journey. So observe, understand, experiment, and let the lessons from the masters guide your artistic evolution.

Chapter 12. Embracing Your Unique Style: Developing Your Artistic Signature

Every artist, through their journey, will come to discover their own distinct style—a unique language through which they communicate their vision to the world. This unique style, or artistic signature, is as individual as your handwriting and as deeply personal as your thoughts. In the evolution of every artist from novice to master, the essential step lies in the development and refinement of this exclusive style. Below, we track this journey, venturing into techniques that can aid in exploring, defining, and embracing your unique style.

12.1. Understanding Personal Style

Before you nurture a style, you need to understand what it is. Personal style, in essence, is the consistently identifiable characteristics, techniques, or themes that make your artwork uniquely yours. It's your voice as an artist, expressed on the canvas. It's frequently an encapsulation of your preferences, experiences, and worldview.

Art style can manifest itself in a myriad of ways. It could be the reiteration of certain themes, favored use of specific color palettes, recurring patterns, preferred structures, or distinctive brushwork. For example, Vincent Van Gogh's kinetic, emotional brushwork or Mondrian's rigid abstraction and focus on primary colors serve as essence of their distinct styles.

Having understood this foundation, let's venture into your journey of discovering and defining your artistic signature.

12.2. Identifying Your Preferences

Start by reflecting on what appeals to you in art. You can begin with analyzing the artworks that inspire you. Make a list of your favorite artists, and identify the specific characteristics of their work that you find intriguing. This exercise will allow you to recognize patterns and elements that resonate with you, which is the first step in defining your own style.

Another useful approach is to review your own past works, if any. Look for recurring themes, similar uses of color, repeated patterns, or particular subjects. These could be key indicators of your instinctive style.

12.3. Experimenting Extensively

The discovery of your style doesn't happen overnight. It involves a lot of exploration and experimentation. Don't restrict yourself to a particular technique, medium, or theme at the initial stages; instead, try out different things

Paint with oils, watercolors, acrylics; sketch with pencils or charcoal. Explore as many different mediums as possible. Delve into abstract art, portraiture, landscape, still life, and more. You'll never know which medium or theme might unveil strengths you weren't aware of, until you attempt it.

12.4. Emphasizing on Self-expression

Art is a means of communication, a translation of your unique thoughts and emotions onto the canvas. Be honest and open in expressing yourself. Don't shy away from showing vulnerability in your art. Authenticity resonates, and your artwork will deeply connect with the audience if it is a true extension of you.

12.5. Refining and Consolidating

Once you've engaged in extensive exploration and experimentation, take time to evaluate your works. Where do you find consistency? What themes or techniques do you seem to keep returning to?

At this point, it's crucial to start refining these elements. Practice them repeatedly, aiming for consistency and mastery. Remember, strengthening your style doesn't entail limiting yourself; instead, it helps define your unique artistic voice.

12.6. Flexibility and Evolution

A style, once developed, isn't rigid. It will naturally evolve over time as you evolve as an artist. This organic evolution of style might emanate from shifts in your life, your perspectives, or your experiences. Ensure you provide enough room for this growth and transformation while embracing your distinctive style.

In conclusion, your artistic signature is deeply connected to you as an individual. So, much like personal growth, its development requires introspection, exploration, learning, refining, and adapting. This journey of establishing your art style is not a sprint, but a marathon, one that intertwines deeply with your journey as an artist. By nurturing this unique style, you will build an artistic identity that's authentically and compellingly yours. Let the world hear your unique artistic voice loud and clear!